This eBook covers the basics of EFT Tapping. For a more complete guide to EFT Tapping, please download "Healing, Transformation, and All Things EFT Tapping" on my website:

www.TessaCason.com

Tessa Cason
5694 Mission Ctr. Rd. #602-213
San Diego, CA. 92108
www.TessaCason.com
Tessa@TessaCason.com

LEGAL NOTICE AND DISCLAIMER:

From author and publisher: The information in this book is not intended to diagnose or treat any particular disease and/or condition. Nothing contained herein is meant to replace qualified medical or psychological advice and/or services. The author and publisher do not assume responsibility for how the reader chooses to apply the techniques herein. Use of the information is at the reader's discretion and discernment. The author and publisher specifically disclaim any and all liability arising directly or indirectly from the use or application contained in this book.

Nothing contained in this book is to be considered medical advice for any specific situation. This information is not intended as a substitute for the advice or medical care of a Physician prior to taking any personal action with respect to the information contained in this book. This book and all of its contents are intended for educational and informational purpose only. The information in this book is believed to be reliable, but is presented without guaranty or warranty.

By reading further, you agree to release the author and publisher from any damages or injury associated with your use of the material in this book.

200 EFT Tapping Statements™ for Wealth

Tessa Cason

Introduction

In 2000, as a Life Coach, I went searching for a tool or technique that could help my clients. Together, the clients and I would decide their homework and the tasks they would complete during the upcoming week. Even though the client knew what to do and wanted to do the tasks, somehow the tasks were not getting completed.

A book on EFT (Emotional Freedom Technique) Tapping was recommended as a potential tool to help my clients. How tapping your head would help my clients, I did not know.

I had some adventuresome clients (and forgiving if need be) that I taught how to tap. When **every single client** returned for their next appointment and shared how different their lives had been that week because of tapping, I took noticed!

I then put all my energy into understanding how tapping worked and how to work EFT.

Our lives don't change until we change the mis-beliefs, the dysfunctional beliefs on a subconscious level. EFT Tapping is one of the most powerful techniques I found that could do just that; change our beliefs on a subconscious level.

Now, EFT Tapping is my main go-to tool to assist my clients in changing the beliefs that prevent them from creating the reality they desire.

Tessa Cason

Table of Contents

Amy's Story

"Amy!" shouted Joy from her office. "Where are the photos for Window #3?"

"In the file, Joy, along with the discussion notes" I said as I approached her office. We go through the same routine for every completed window display and I have been here a year! I stood in the doorway and waited for Joy to look up. She never does so I said, "If you don't need me, I think I will take my break now."

Joy's glasses slid down her nose as she looked up and said, "No. I don't need you." Then the disheveled head, with every curl out of place that could be, went back to whatever she was working on.

As I walked to the breakroom, I surveyed the floor displays while pondering the state of my life. My thoughts drifted to Joy, my job, my unhappiness doing my job, and more unpleasant work stuff. "Joy" is my boss's name and she is anything but joyful to work for.

After I graduated from high school, I looked for a job for a solid year! I either lacked the experience or the education needed. I felt like I was in a vicious cycle, spinning round and round and round. Finally I was hired at the large chain store. I have worked in several departments over the last 8 years and, because of my art background, this last year I had been working as Joy's assistant or, should I say, Joy's apprentice.

"I think Joy has been dressing windows since the beginning of visual merchandising" I grumbled as I entered the breakroom. Seldom is the breakroom empty, yet it was today. Usually there is someone in the room. After all, this is a large chain store with lots of employees.

The morning paper was spread out on the table. I sat down and started to flip through the pages, looking at the various display ads. I know, people usually read the paper for the content. I peruse the paper and study everything about ads: the layout, message, graphics, font style, font size.

Turning page after page, analyzing the display ads, I stopped on the Announcement page. There, on the page, was a photo of my biology lab partner, Judy Ross. She was joining her dad's law firm. I really liked Judy. She was a Varsity Cheerleader, Senior Class President, honor student, voted 'Most Likely to Succeed,' and a really sweet girl. We laughed a lot at our blunders in biology lab.

"Wow," I thought. "I'm working in a chain store and Judy has graduated from college, law school, both with honors and distinction, and is now a partnership with her dad in a law firm." A wave of exhaustion and sadness swept through my body. "Judy is an attorney and I'm a poorly paid apprentice to an absentminded, uncommunicative woman would couldn't make it as an artist and now is my boss. On my salary, I can't even afford to move out of my parents' house!"

The rest of the day, my thoughts focused on what Judy had accomplished and what I had not. Her successes in high school continued. My "nothingness" continued after high school. While preparing dinner with my mom that night, I shared the announcement I saw in the paper about Judy.

"Oh, speaking of high school," my mom said. "There was a 'Save the Date' postcard in the mail today for you for your 10-year reunion."

Again, I felt a wave of exhaustion and sadness rippled though my body. I saw down at the kitchen table and softly started to cry. My loving, confused Mom dried her hands with her apron and sat down next to me, brushing away the tears. With a concerned look on her face as tears rolled down my cheeks she said, "What is it, Amy? You don't have to go to the reunion if you don't want to."

"Mom, you made me an offer several months ago after we attended the EFT Tapping class," I said.

"Oh, yes, I remember," my mom said, reflecting back. "Great teacher. Great class. I still tap just about every day. I remember telling you that if you wanted to see her privately, your day and I would pay for a couple of visits. Is that the offer you are referring to?"

Looking down at my hands resting on the table, I looked up at my mom and said, "I really liked her. She seemed knowledgeable, compassionate, and funny. I haven't tapped since the class," my voice trailed off as the tears welled up.

My efficient mom stood up, walked over to the computer, and started clicking the keys. I followed her to the computer. A colorful website came up on the computer as I sat next to her. We saw the photo of a smiling Sarah and my mom said, "She offers packages. As your birthday present, your dad and I will pay for a package of sessions."

Money did not flow in our home. Both my parents had to work really hard and were barely scraping by. I happily paid them rent and several times a week came home from work with bags of groceries.

"Oh, Mom," I whispered. "It's okay. I can figure this out on my own. That's too much to ask. I'm okay, really I am."

Well, that didn't go over too well with my mom. "Amy Anderson. Are you telling me how to spend my money?" she said with a sharpness in the tone of her voice.

A little shocked, I sat up straight and stared at my mom. This was not my mom. Normally she is comforting and nurturing. This woman acted as if I had insulted her. "Mom, you can't afford to pay for a package for me," I responded. "I'm okay. Really I am, just a rough day at work. That's all. I will be fine tomorrow."

"Amy, of my three kids, you are the smartest and most capable. Your dad and I felt shame that we could not afford to pay for a college education," she said with a softer tone.

"Mom," I said. "I never expected you to pay for college."
"Now that your brothers are out of the house and supporting themselves and you are paying us rent, money isn't as tight. We've been able to save some money. Your father and I have actually talked about your unhappiness at work."

With compassion in her voice she continued, "I can't help you, but maybe Sarah can. It's hard for a mom to see her only daughter unhappy. I feel so helpless not knowing what I can do to help you. This is the only way I know to help. Sessions with Sarah can be your birthday and early Christmas present." Cheerily she added, "This way we don't have to play 20 questions to find out what you want for Christmas!"

I hugged my mom, gave her a kiss on her cheek, and, smiling I said, "Can you hand me the phone, please?"

My mom said, "I will even dial the number." She pulled up Sarah's number on the website and handed me the phone after dialing.

After the call ended, I smiled at my mom and said, "Sarah remembered the mother-daughter duo in her class. I'm surprised. I guess we made an impression. I have an appointment next week." I paused and said with genuine love in my voice, "Mom, I love you and thank you."

At the appointed hour, I walked into Sarah's waiting room. Before I could sit down, Sarah greeted me and we walked to her office together. As we sat down, Sarah said, "Your mom called the day after you booked your appointment and paid for a package. She said it was your birthday present. Happy birthday. What a wonderful and thoughtful gift," said Sarah.

"I do have a great mom. It's not my birthday quite yet," I said.

"I feel honored that you would want sessions with me as your birthday gift," said Sarah with humility. "Hopefully, I can provide some insight into your life and the issues at hand. Have a seat and let's get started."

Sarah's office felt warm and comforting. She had various framed charts on the walls including David Hawkins' Map of Consciousness, the EFT Tapping points, and others on symbolism. I immediately felt comfortable and hopeful.

Sarah started with, "What brings you into my office today? What's going on that you want to heal?"

I thought for a few seconds then answered, "I don't know exactly. I'm not happy at work." Pondering my statement I said, "I think I am waiting to start my life after I am happy. I don't think I have started my life yet."

"That sounds like a new thought," Sarah said, "waiting to start your life after being happy."

"I think it is. I mean I guess I knew it but never verbalized it," I said reflectively.

"Can you tell me more?" asked an interested Sarah.

With a heavy sigh, I started, "I have two older brothers. My parents couldn't afford to send any of us to college. My two older brothers went to trade schools. One is now a mechanic and the other does construction. My parents love having a mechanic and handyman in the family. Anything goes wrong, they call one of the boys," I said with a laugh.

I continued, "Then there is me. For eight years I have worked at the big chain store. I have worked in several different departments. I am now in the visual merchandising division working for an absentminded woman named Joy. It is not joyful working with Joy."

Sarah asked, "What created the push to seek counseling?"

"Well, two things I guess," I answered. "I haven't been happy at the big chain store or working with Joy. Last week when I was on my break, I was perusing the paper analyzing ads and came across an announcement in the paper that my biology lab partner, Judy Ross, had joined her dad's law firm. She was very successful in high school and apparently in college as well, graduating with honors. She has completed college, law school, passing the bar the first time she took the exam, and is now an attorney. I work at a chain store."

"And the second," asked Sarah.

Feeling exhausted and sad again, with another heavy sigh, I said, "The second was a 'Save the Date' postcard I received the same day for my high school's 10th annual reunion. I can't believe that I graduated from high school nearly 10 years ago. It seems just like yesterday. Judy has accomplished so much in the last 10 years and I have not."

Sarah started laughing and said, "Well, that must be heavy. With a deep sigh, you slid down in your chair as if invisible weights were pulling you down."

"Exactly," I exclaimed! "That's exactly how I feel. I feel weighted down by invisible weights. I don't know what's pulling me down. I feel exhausted. I feel as if I am moving through mud!"

"Great visual," commented Sarah. "There are four elements: air, fire, water, and earth. Air is the intellect. Fire is our energy. Water represents the emotions and earth is our grounding. Mud is too much water for the earth."

"I get it," I said with insight. "My emotions are drowning out my grounding or something like that, right?"

"Exactly, mud is an overabundance of water in regard to earth. Water represents our emotions. So, yes, your emotions are creating mud. Very slippery to walk **on** mud plus it's difficult to walk **through** mud," Sarah added.

"That's exactly how I feel. My daily life feels like I am walking through mud and it's exhausting. Any hope for me?" I asked playfully. "Why is it that some people soar, like Judy, and others of us trudge through mud?"

"The answer may surprise you. It's only one word," Sarah said. "Beliefs. Everything in our life is a result of our beliefs. All of our thoughts and feelings, our choices and decisions, and our actions and reactions are based on our beliefs."

"Sounds simple, yet in reality, in real life, day-to-day living, it isn't so simple," I commented.

"No, it's not," said Sarah agreeing with me then asked. "It sounds like you want to begin looking at your work situation. Is this about right?"

"I'm not sure if it's work or money. Money always seems to be in short supply. Between rent, food, gas, insurance, there never seems to be any left over for fun stuff." Then I added, "It's a drag having to support one's self."

She laughed at my drag comment. Laughter is good I imagine. I just don't seem to have a lot of laughter in my life at this time, I thought.

Sarah said, "Let's dive in. Let's review the tapping, how it works, how to tap, and answer any questions you might have about tapping."

After we reviewed, Sarah said that work was a subset of money and wealth. She thought the place to begin was my feelings about money, having money, not having money, how I felt about money, and then we would deal with the beliefs in the next session. I glanced at the clock and realized that the end of the session was approaching quickly. "Wow, that time went fast," I thought.

Before the session ended, Sarah wrote out 15 tapping statements for me to tap on my own as my homework. "I have one other assignment for you between now and when we meet again. I want you to think about your dream job would be, regardless if you are qualified or not to do the job."

When I walked through the door at the end of the day, I gave my mother a huge hug. She asked if the session went well.

"Mom, this is the first time I have felt hopeful in regard to money," I told her excitedly. "Sarah gave me homework. I have these 15 tapping statements I have to tap this week, and between now and next week I have to come up with my dream job."

Her mom beamed from ear to ear and said, "Amy, I can tap with you. I think I can benefit from the tapping as well. How many were there?"

"Fifteen," I told her. Excitedly, I added, "I would love it if you tapped with me. What if we do five a night for the next three nights?"

"That works for me. What's the other part of the homework?" added my mom.

"What would be my dream job," I answered. "I've never thought about what my dream job would be. I only know what I don't want, which is what I have now."

"You are so talented, Amy. You can be anything you want to be," her mom remarked.

"You're my mom. You're supposed to say that and it's not true. I will give it some thought though," I said reflectively.

For the next week, Amy and her mom tapped after dinner. Amy started journaling her thoughts of what she might want to do. She still had no idea what her dream job would be when she returned for her second session with Sarah.

Sarah thought we should tap before we ventured into the discussion.

* It's not okay for me to have my dream job.
* It's not okay for me to be paid what I am worth.
* It's not okay for me to depend on myself for my income.
* I will be disappointed when I fail at my dream job.
* It's not okay for me to rise above my circumstances.
* I don't have the power to create the reality I desire.
* I can have my needs met but not my wants.
* I don't have the courage to be rich.

I told Sarah, "I didn't realize this question would be so tough. My whole focus this week has been this question and I have no answer after a week! I am very disappointed in myself."

"Wow," said Sarah. "Reframing. You don't know your dream job yet. 'Yet' is the operative word here. Some people never know what their dream job is. They stay in jobs they hate year after year after year."

With a sigh and a tear, I told Sarah I had been one of those people for the last eight years. But, I didn't want more of the same. With her help, maybe I could change that around. And with that, she gave me more homework. Part of my homework was to journal about whether I had the courage to be rich, to be empowered, and to live a life that fulfilled me.

"Wow...heavy duty," I thought. That night when I shared the session with my mom, I told her I didn't think I had the courage to be rich or empowered. Maybe that's why I couldn't figure out my dream job. This was getting much harder than I thought it would be. I could feel my fears surfacing. I told my mom I should probably quit the sessions since I did not want to waste their money if I couldn't do the work.

My mom said, "Absolutely not! You have never been a quitter and just because the going is getting tough isn't an indication it's time to quit. Instead, it's time to do more tapping and to trust the process."

When my mom spoke like that, you did not dare back down. It was full steam ahead with her. She never backed down from a challenge. And actually that conversation ended up being a turning point for me. My mom and I continued to tap. The more we tapped, the more both of us found our courage to be empowered and to be rich.

The sessions with Sarah continued. I could feel I was improving each week. I knew that my passion was art. My mom knew her passion was designing clothing and sewing. We both attended free classes at the continuing education school. I found that I had a passion for designing websites. Who would have guessed? Not me.

In the web design class, I learned how to plan, design, and build a website. A class assignment was to build a website for someone else. I approached Joy and asked if she would like a website to promote and sell her artwork. I was surprised at her response. She didn't think she had the courage to put her artwork out in the world. I gave her 24 hours to think about it. She came into work the next day revitalized. She said she would do it. She had just created some new pieces that no one had seen.

My mom started designing children's clothes and selling them on eBay. In one of my classes, I needed to design and build a website for eCommerce. How perfect to have a mother who was starting her own business. Her clothing was successfully selling on eBay. Together we designed her eCommerce website.

In my advanced web design and development class, I was to create another website. No one else I knew needed a website. My mom suggested that I contact Judy Ross and see if Judy and her dad needed a website for their law practice. I feel very intimidated by my mom's suggestion and decided I needed to address this with Sarah at my next session.

"Sarah, the web designing is continuing to be fun and I have found my passion," I said. Taking a deep breath I continued, "In my current class, I have a class project to create a website for a real person. I couldn't come up with anyone so my mom suggested Judy Ross, my high school biology lab partner. I feel so intimidated. She is so accomplished and I am not."

"What I think I hear you saying, Amy, is that you feel 'less than.' Is this about right?" asked Sarah.

"Yup. That would sum it up," I said feeling embarrassed. "'Less than.' I have felt less than my whole life, from the get-go. I see other people soaring and accomplishing great things and instead of soaring, I flounder." My eyes were misting over again.

"Amy, what you have described is survival. When we are caught in survival, it is difficult to thrive. We can only survive. Feeling 'less than' and anxiety are ever present. The fight-flight-freeze mode is always on," said Sarah.

"Can I heal this feeling of 'less than'?" I asked hopeful.

With a smile, Sarah said, "Yes. Let's get started."

With that said, Sarah and I looked at the beliefs I had around survival. Again, my mom and I tapped the homework. After tapping and my confidence increased, I called Judy and was put through to her. To my great surprised and shock, she remembered me. She asked if I wanted to have tea sometime. With excitement, I said yes.

When we met the next day, I shared with Judy how her accomplishments had become my motivation to change my life.

With a genuine smile on her face, she said, "Amy, you may not remember but for biology lab, when I came into the lab, I deliberately sat next to you so we could be partners. Of everyone in the class, you were my first choice."

My jaw dropped with surprised. Still stunned, I said, "I thought you had to settle for me as your partner."

Laughing, Judy said, "No. I thought you would have thought I was arrogant if I told you I had wanted you as a lab partner."

Both Judy and I had a wonderful time that morning. It was the first time I truly felt her equal and that she wasn't better than me. I didn't feel less than. I shared with her my new career path and asked if she and her dad had thought about launching a website. She had. She was trying to bring her dad into the 21st century. She wanted to blog and share with others ways in which they could protect their assets.

"You know, Amy," said Judy, "the class reunion is coming up soon. For your class project, what if you created a website for the reunion? If that goes well, I think by then I can talk my dad into a website."

The following month, my mom attended my final session with me. Sitting across from Sarah, my mom said, "Little did I know that, when I offered sessions with you as Amy's birthday and Christmas gift, how much my life would transform. I tapped every statement you gave Amy for her homework. I took classes on turning your love of sewing into a business and now have more orders than I can fill. I quit my day job and now my focus is creating personalized outfits for children all day long. It is a thrill for me when the parents and grandparents email me photos of children dressed in my outfits. Me!"

Beaming with pride my mom added, "Children are wearing the outfits that I designed and made. I can't believe that I found my dream job." I hugged my mom as tears filled her eyes.

I took a deep breath, sat up tall, and shared my news with Sarah. "Amy's dad was so impressed with the website I created for the class reunion Judy didn't have to twist his arm. I created a website for their law practice."

Sarah smiled as she listened to our successes.

I continued, "At the class reunion, I reconnected with people that I thought didn't much like me in high school. I was surprised that I had a great time. Being able to connect, truly connect, with my high school classmates, I realized my embarrassment in high school was about me, how I felt less than everyone else. Healing and tapping on the survival issue, I can feel myself soar. I truly am thriving," I said with a smile on my face.

"And," I continued. "Several people at the reunion loved the website I created for the reunion and have hired me to design and build their websites. I quit my chain store job. Last week I moved into a little studio that has a great view that inspires me creatively. I am truly happy."

"I am very happy for both of you," Sarah said. "Each of you did the work, did the tapping, and now has created your dream job. Let's do some tapping to make sure it is okay for both of you to soar and thrive."

At the end of the session, my mom and I hugged Sarah and thanked her for facilitating the changes in our lives.

Intro to Wealth

The dictionary defines "abundance" as
1. A great or plentiful amount.
2. Fullness to an overflowing quantity.
3. Affluence; wealth.

"Wealth" is defined as
1. A large amount of money and valuable material possessions.
2. The state of being rich.
3. A great profusion.

"Rich" is defined as
1. Possessing great material wealth, an abundant supply.
2. Having great worth or value.
3. Magnificent, meaningful, and significant.

Abundance, wealth, richness are about plentiful amounts and worth. Financial wealth is only one aspect of abundance.

* What we manifest in our lives is a direct result of our beliefs.

* Our beliefs determine our thoughts and feelings which in turn determine our choices and decisions.

> If we are happy and joyful, we will see happiness in everything.
> If we are fearful, we will see fear around every corner.
> If we have a mentality of wealth and abundance, we will prosper.

* Our beliefs determine the level of our wealth and abundance.

The quality of *seeds* we plant and the amount of *weeding* we do will determine the amount of abundance we create for ourselves.

The seeds are our beliefs, thoughts, dreams, integrity, and our goals.

Weeding is removing the dysfunctional beliefs, emotions, and thoughts that prevent us from manifesting abundance.

Healing our Wealth, Prosperity, Abundance Issue

Our dysfunctional beliefs are like a scratch on a vinyl record. Every time we try to move beyond the scratch, we are thrown back and are not allowed to move beyond the scratch. Lack of prosperity is a scratch in the vinyl record.

Power of 3: Issue – Cause – Effect

For every issue, there is a cause and an effect. To heal and move beyond the scratch in the vinyl record, we need to heal all three: the issue, the cause, and result of or the effect of the cause.

It is difficult to be prosperous when we are stuck in survival. When we are stuck in survival we feel disempowered to thrive. We can only survive. It takes Courage to step into our Personal Power and to Succeed.

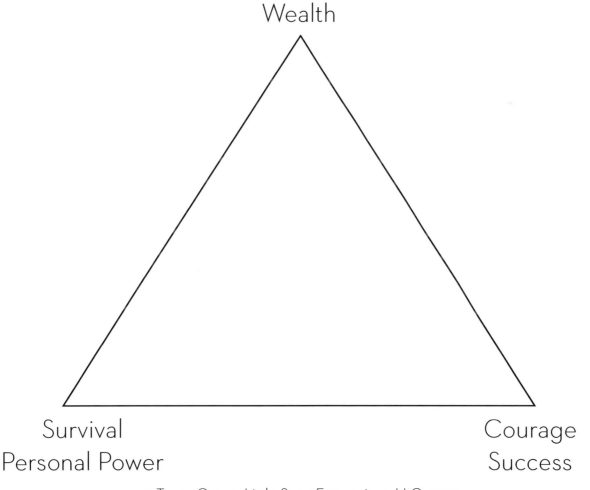

Wealth

Survival
Personal Power

Courage
Success

Prosperity, Abundance, Money, Wealth Intro

Money never starts an idea. It is the idea that starts the money.

W. J. Cameron

Abundance is the natural state of affairs in the Universe. Experiencing less than total abundance is a reflection of not aligning ourselves with universal principles, not remaining in present time, and our dysfunctional beliefs.

Universal Laws are underlying principles that exist in our Universe, everywhere, worldwide. They are eternal, ever present, and absolute. Universal laws are not subject to change. They exist and influence our lives whether we are aware of them or not. Universal Laws operate on all levels: physical, mental, and spiritual. One such law is the Law of Gravity. It is eternal and absolute and will not change in our Universe or at least, will not change as long as we are standing on Earth. Gravity exists and influences our lives.

By understanding Universal Laws and aligning ourselves with them, we will be aligning ourselves with the Power of the Universe. Below is a discussion on the Law of Growth, the Law of Attraction, the Law of Manifestation, the Law of Action, the Law of Cause and Effect, and the Law of Gratitude/Appreciation.

The **Law of Growth** is about the complex process of evolution, how we evolve, and grow. It is not as simple as planting seeds and harvesting the crop. It is also about where we plant the seeds, the conditions of the soil, weather, and climate, how much sun, water, and nourishment the seeds receive. It is also about removing the weeds on a regular basis.

* The *seeds* are our beliefs and our thoughts.

* Our beliefs and thoughts define *the essence* of who we are and how we will live our lives.

* Our dreams define the *destination,* where we would like to end up.

* The goals define the *route* we take to reach our dreams.

* Our beliefs, thoughts, and integrity define the *journey.*

For example, let's say you enjoy everything about music...playing, composing, and singing. Your dream is to be involved with music somehow. After much exploration, you decide you want to teach music to children.

* The dream of being involved with music led to the goal of teaching private music lessons to children.

* Your thoughts and beliefs will define the journey. Thoughts like, "How do I acquire students" and beliefs such as, "I can't market myself" will define the path, the route to the destination of teaching private music lessons to children.

* The weeds would be the dysfunctional, mis-beliefs that prevent us from reaching our dreams. Using the same example of teaching private music lessons to children:

* "No one will want to learn from me."

* "I don't have the skill and talents needed to teach music."

* "I will never be able to support myself teaching music."

In order to succeed at teaching private music lessons, the weeds, the dysfunctional beliefs that would prevent the success of this venture, need to be identified and removed. [EFT Tapping is a very effective method of removing the weeds.]

The **Law of Growth** is about learning from our mistakes, our experiences, and everything that surrounds us. A *New York Times* reporter asked Thomas Edison after his 700th unsuccessful attempt at inventing the electric light, "How does it feel to have failed 700 times?" Mr. Edison responded, "I have not failed 700 times. I have not failed once. I have succeeded in proving that those 700 ways will not work. When I have eliminated the ways that will not work, I will find the way that will work."

We start to die when we stop growing and learning.

The **Law of Attraction** states "like" energies are attracted to and are drawn together. Like attracts like. Our thoughts and beliefs are the magnets that draw to us "like" energies. If our thoughts are of poverty and lack, poverty and lack is what we will attract into our lives. To attract abundance, we need to have thoughts of abundance. What we focus on expands.

The **Law of Manifestation** states that everything we want to create or manifest begins with an intention, an idea, and/or a thought. The intention and desire begins the process of manifesting wealth in our lives.

Having a dream, setting intention, defining the goal, and making a detailed plan is not enough to manifest the dream or the goal. We have to take action. This brings us to the **Law of Action**. We must take action toward that which we want to manifest. Planning, setting goals, reading books, researching are all part of the beginning stages. The next step is to implement the plan, take the first action toward the goals, and/or try one or more ideas our research uncovered.

Brian Tracy says: "The most important key to achieving great success is to decide upon your goal and launch, get started, take action, move. All successful people men and women are big dreamers. They imagine what their future could be, ideal in every respect, and then take some action every day toward that goal. Once we start, everything changes. New avenues and opportunities open up for us, openings that we could not have seen had we not been in forward motion."

The **Law of Cause and Effect** states that every action produces a reaction. All of our actions are based on our beliefs. If we have a belief that we will never be prosperous, the end result will be, we will never be prosperous. The seeds we sow today are the harvest of tomorrow.

The **Law of Gratitude and Appreciation**. What we focus on expands. When we are appreciative of what we have, it grows. Gratitude and Appreciation bring us into present time, out of our fear and anger, our disappointments and our anxieties.

We can only heal when we are in present time. We can only manifest when we are present. We can only grow when we take full responsibility for our lives. Gratitude and appreciation is a necessary step in the process of manifesting prosperity in our lives.

How do we manifest and create in our lives the abundance and prosperity we desire?

1. Set the intention.

2. Examine the current circumstances of our lives. What are we attracting into our life? What "like" energy is most dominant?

3. Determine the beliefs that are creating the current circumstances.

4. Delete those beliefs that won't advance us toward abundance.

5. Add new beliefs that empower and support our intentions.

We will be presented with opportunities and challenges to heal all the beliefs, thoughts, and feelings that prevent us from manifesting the abundance we desire. Hold on. The ride could get bumpy.

Survival Intro

The role of the physical body is to keep us alive. The body breathes for us, pumps our heart for us, regulates our body temperature, digests our food, and converts the food into energy. All without conscious thought.

The role of the physical body is to keep us safe. When our hand gets too close to a flame, the body automatically pulls the hand back to safety. When our face is submerged in water, our body stops breathing to prevent the body from inhaling water. All without conscious thought.

The role of the physical body is to keep us alive and safe. When it perceives anything as a threat, the body automatically goes into SURVIVAL MODE, FIGHT-FLIGHT-FREEZE, to prepare us to either fight, run away, or play dead. The body begins to breathe faster. Our awareness is heightened. The pulse and heart rate quickens. Survival mode is automatic...without conscious thought.

All of the above is automatic...without conscious thought. We don't have to tell the body to breathe. It knows we need air. We don't tell the body to heighten our awareness when threatened. It knows we are in danger.

Dr. John Montgomery says, "Biologically and evolutionarily, all 'negative' or distressing, emotions, like fear, disgust, or anxiety, can be thought of as 'survival-mode' emotions: they signal to the body and brain that our survival and well-being may be at risk."

Distressing emotions such as fear alerts the physical body that our survival may be at risk. When we feel fearful, the physical body automatically, without conscious thought, goes into survival mode.

In survival mode, the rational mind disengages. Fear is valued. We use anger to keep people at a safe distance. We become hyper-vigilant. We are constantly on edge. Our guard is always up. Fear, anger, depression, anxiety, and avoidance become our constant companions. We are only able to focus on the immediate tasks at hand.

Long-range goals are not even on the horizon. The ability to interact with other people is risky. Relaxing could mean death. Enjoying life and thriving is not possible. Positive emotions such as love, joy, serenity, happiness, and hope do not exist.

In survival mode, the survival emotions of fear, anger, and anxiety flood the body. We view the world through the veil of fear.

Conversely, this is as well...when we are experiencing distressing emotions such as fear, anger, anxiety, shame, and/or self-pity, this can throw us into survival mode.

Courage Intro

It takes a lot of courage to release the familiar and seemingly secure, to embrace the new. There is no real security in what is no longer meaningful. There is more security in the adventurous and exciting. In movement there is life. In change there is power.

Alan Cohen

Courage is defined as "mental or moral strength to venture, persevere, and withstand danger, fear, or difficulty." It is derived from the Latin *cor*, which means heart.

What would we need courage for? Well, here are a few:

* Being emotionally courageous, living our lives with integrity, truthfulness, and awareness.

* Being present, in our body, totally and completely in the moment.

* To experience emotions, yet not to be controlled by our emotions: to face our fears, our hurts, and not to be controlled by them.

* To be successful. It is easy to fail. The challenge is in succeeding.

* To find peace in a world full of conflict and bullies. The world is a place of constant conflict with people against people, nations against nations. The world is full of bullies that use intimidation and control to hide their insecurities and fears.

* To be loved and to love, to accept love and to give love, to be vulnerable and accepting of ourselves as well as others.

* To forgive. Forgiveness is a gift we give to ourselves, for ourselves, so we can continue on with our lives. Yet in the middle of the pain, we don't want to forgive. Think of forgiving as having compassion.

* To be part of a team, to be a team player. Teamwork does not come easy to those who want to control and be in charge.

* To be the architects of our lives, to have dreams and goals, and to work toward their fulfillment.

* To be whole, to integrate physically, mentally, emotionally, and spiritually into one whole being.

Personal Power Intro

It is not who we are that holds us back. It is who we think we are not.

Michael Nolan

Personal Power is not about physical, brute strength. It is not about having a huge financial net worth. It is not about the number and height of our successes and accomplishments. It is not about the number of people we control or our personal influence. It is not about fame, the house we live in, the car we drive, or the clothes we wear. It is not about political muscle, either.

Personal power is the strength, substance, and character of our inner being. It is about living our lives in Truth. Personal power is the discernment to know the difference between Truth and true. It is knowing that, whatever life throws at us, we will prevail. Personal power is about learning and growing. It is the appreciation for All That Is.

As a working, single mom, Tiffany did the best she could raising her daughter Summer, who was now nearing the tween years. Six months previously, she had moved the two of them into the home of her boyfriend. Everything was going well...until the night she came home early to find her boyfriend molesting her daughter. At that instant, she grabbed her daughter, ran out the door, called the police, and took her daughter to the nearest hospital.

In an instant, Tiffany's and Summer's lives were changed forever. Working paycheck to paycheck, the financial resources were not immediately available to find a new home. She had to ask friends and family for assistance and support...a humbling experience for Tiffany. The situation stripped Tiffany of her self-confidence, her ability to trust others was shaken, and daily she suffered the shame of creating an unsafe environment for her daughter.

Yet, she realized she had a choice. She could be the victim, feel sorry for herself, or she could take responsibility. Tiffany took a deep breath and surrendered to what was, the current situation she found herself in. Surrendering taught her about acceptance; needing assistance from others taught her to be open to receive. She was grateful and surprised by the kindness of others and their willingness to help when she needed their help the most.

"This event shook me to my core," Tiffany said. "It was a huge wake-up call, a realization that I needed to live my life in Truth. I realized that the events themselves were neutral. What was important was my response to the events. I knew I didn't want more of what I had. My desire was for change so I could manifest a different life. It took mindful awareness, sometimes moment to moment, of how each choice felt to me. I had to weigh each against the idea if I put this out into the Universe, is this what I want back? This daily, sometimes hourly, practice of constantly assessing and experimenting brought me great confidence and faith in my ability to handle anything. This gave me a tremendous amount of personal power."

After reflecting on her story, she added, "Knowing that I had the power of choice created a sense of peace for me. Though cash was in short supply, I felt blessed and abundant as a result of the generosity and graciousness of others. I'm not sure if this means my character was being revealed or if the experience built my character."

Actually, a little of both happened. Her character was being revealed and the experience did build her character. Someone with a victim mentality would have continued to be a victim. Tiffany chose to grow, learn, and evolve by this event rather than to be helpless. She tuned within to her inner compass, the compass that leads to healing and well-being.

My Top 45 Qualities of Personal Power:

Acceptance
Accountable
Allowing
Awareness
Belief in self
Clear, sharp mind
Commitment
Communicator
Compassionate
Confident
Congruent
Conscious
Courageous
Determination
Diplomacy
Discernment
Emotionally strong
Emotionally mature
Empowers others
Follow-through
Giving
Gracious
Gratitude
Grounded
Imaginative
Insightful
Integrity
Kind
Listening
Observant
On purpose with life
Passionate

Perceptive
Perseverance
Persistent
Physically fit
Reliable
Resilient
Respectful
Responsible
Sets goals
Teach by Example
Warm
Willingness
Wisdom

Success Intro

Those on top of the mountain did not fall there.

Marcus Washling

To each of us, success is different. Yet, there are common threads throughout all successes. Here are some of the common threads:

Successful people:

* Know what they want.

* Allow themselves to dream.

* Set goals and work toward their fulfillment.

* Have a detailed plan to accomplish their goals and dreams.

* Take action.

* Understand that setbacks and obstacles will teach them valuable lessons.

* Focus on solutions and are solution-oriented.

* Know everything they accomplish in life is up to them.

* Take complete responsibility for their lives.

* Don't quit or give up.

* Understand there is no guarantee they will succeed.

* Are flexible about the process of achieving their goals.

* Make decisions and continue to move forward.

* Continually reevaluate their plan.

* Are committed to the fulfillment of their dreams and goals.

* Are resilient and persistent.

* Accept change and adapt to difficulties.

* Believe in their success before success is visible.

* Are willing to accept feedback and self-correct.

* Live in the "now." They are present in their lives.

* Know that life is not a rehearsal for something else.

* Understand the seeds they plant today will be the rewards they will harvest tomorrow.

* Expect to meet many obstacles and difficulties along the way.

* Know that failure is only temporary, just part of the process.

* Pick themselves up after failure and press on.

Successful people are dreamers with their feet firmly planted in reality. The challenge of working toward their dreams and goals is just as exciting as the fulfillment of them. Overcoming each obstacle strengthens their resolve. Each lesson they learn from failure brings them closer to success. Their focus is on the goal. Successful people know they will succeed before there is evidence of their success.

How Do We Transform Our Lives to Be Wealthy

We transform our lives by identifying and removing the dysfunctional beliefs that prevents us being wealthy. To remove the dysfunctional beliefs, we need a powerful tool to do so. One such tool is EFT Tapping.

This eBook only covers the basics of EFT Tapping. For a more thorough information, please visit www.TessaCason and download the FREE eBook on Healing, Transformation, and All Things EFT Tapping.

In this eBook I have 40 tapping statements for each topic - Wealth, Survival, Courage, Personal Power, and Success, 200 Tapping Statements. The full version of this eBook with 1,000 EFT Tapping Statements can be found in my store on my website: www.TessaCason.com.

Beliefs and the Subconscious Mind

Everything in our life is a direct result of our beliefs.

A belief is a mental acceptance of and conviction in the truth, actuality, or validity of something. It is what we believe to be true, whether it is Truth or not. A belief is a thought that influences energy all the time.

A mis-belief, a dysfunctional belief is a belief that takes us away from peace, love, joy, stability, acceptance, and harmony. It causes us to feel stressed, fearful, anxious, and/or insecure.

The reason we aren't successful, happy, or prosperous has to do with our beliefs. Our beliefs determine our thoughts and feelings. Our thoughts and feelings determine our choices and decisions as well as our actions and reactions. Beliefs, then, precede all of our thoughts, feelings, choices, decisions, actions, reactions, and experiences.

Beliefs **precede** all of our thoughts, feelings, decisions, choices, actions, reactions, and experiences...

Our beliefs **determine** our thoughts.
Our thoughts **determine** our feelings.
Our thoughts and feelings **determine** our choices and decisions.
Our thoughts and feelings **determine** our actions and reactions.

Can you determine someone's beliefs from their actions and reactions? Persons A, B, C, and D just received a compliment that they looked nice today.

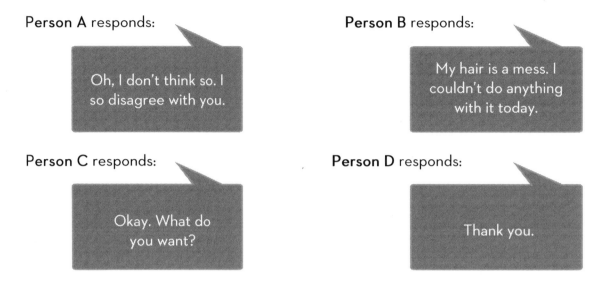

Person A responds:

> Oh, I don't think so. I so disagree with you.

Person B responds:

> My hair is a mess. I couldn't do anything with it today.

Person C responds:

> Okay. What do you want?

Person D responds:

> Thank you.

Person A: Totally disagrees. They don't think they look nice today. Person A definitely has self-esteem and self-worth issues. When we are not able to accept a compliment, it's a slap in the face for the person giving the compliment. It's as if Person A is saying, "If you think I look nice, your opinion sucks."

Person B: Cannot nor will not accept the compliment. They defect the compliment with a reason why they couldn't look nice. They justify their reason for not accepting the compliment. Think there might be a little bit of anger and/or shame in this type of response?

Person C: They think there are strings attached to the compliment. Anyone that would compliment them must want something. Might trust and discernment be an issue for them?

Person D: Well, if the response is genuine, then we know they have a healthy self-esteem and self-worth. If the response was said with arrogance, like "Naturally I look nice today" then we could either have someone who really is arrogant or someone who is insecure and using arrogance to hide the insecurity.

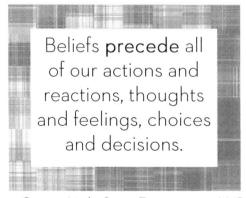

Beliefs **precede** all of our actions and reactions, thoughts and feelings, choices and decisions.

Subconscious Mind

The Conscious Mind

The conscious mind is that part of us that thinks, passes judgements, makes decisions, remembers, analyzes, has desires, and communicates with others. It is responsible for logic and reasoning, understanding and comprehension. The mind determines our actions, feelings, thoughts, judgements, and decisions **based on the beliefs.**

The Subconscious Mind

The subconscious is the part of the mind that is responsible for all of our involuntary actions like heart beat and breathing rate. It does not evaluate, make decisions, or pass judgment. It just is. It does not determine if something is "right" or "wrong."

The subconscious is much like the software of a computer. On the computer keyboard, if we press the key for the letter "a," we will see the letter "a" on the screen, even though we may have wanted to see "t."

Just as a computer can only do what it has been programmed to do, we can only do as we are programmed to do. Our programming is determined by our beliefs.

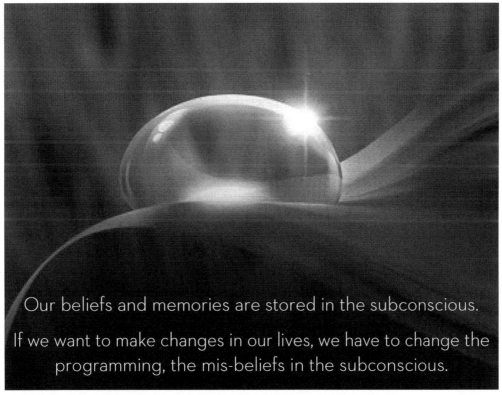

Our beliefs and memories are stored in the subconscious.

If we want to make changes in our lives, we have to change the programming, the mis-beliefs in the subconscious.

3 Rules of the Subconscious Mind

Three rules of the subconscious mind include:

1. Personal. It only understands "I," "me," "myself." First person.

2. Positive. The subconscious does not hear the word "no." When you say, "I am not going to eat that piece of cake," the subconscious mind hears "Yummm! Cake! I am going to eat a piece of that cake!"

3. Present time. Time does not exist for the subconscious. The only time it knows is "now," present time. "I'm going to start my diet tomorrow." "Tomorrow" never comes thus the diet is never started.

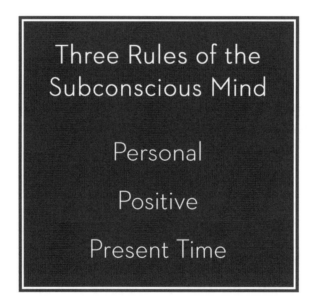

Three Rules of the
Subconscious Mind

Personal

Positive

Present Time

EFT Tapping – Emotional Freedom Technique

If we want to make changes in our lives, long-lasting, permanent, constructive changes, we have to change the destructive, dysfunctional, mis-beliefs in the subconscious. We have to change the programming in the subconscious.

EFT Tapping changes dysfunctional, mis-beliefs on a subconscious level.

What is EFT – Emotional Freedom Technique:

EFT is a technique that allows us to change dysfunctional beliefs and emotions on a subconscious level. It involves making a statement while tapping different points along meridian paths.

The general principle behind EFT is that the cause of all negative emotions is a disruption in the body's energy system. By tapping on locations where a number of the different meridians flow, we are able to release unproductive memories, emotions, and beliefs which cause the blockages.

EFT Tapping Statements:

An EFT statement has three parts to it:

Part 1: Starts with "**Even though,**" followed by

Part 2: A statement which could be the **dysfunctional emotion or belief**, and

Part 3: Ends with "**I totally and completely accept myself.**"

A total statement would be "**Even though, I crave sweets, I totally and completely accept myself.**"

The instructions below are described if you were using your right hand. Reverse directions to tap using the left hand. It is only necessary to tap one side. Tapping both sides does not add any additional benefit.

I. Begin with circling or the Karate Chop Point (See next page):

A. With the fingertips of your right hand, find a tender spot below your left collar bone. Once you have found the tender spot, with your right fingertips, press firmly on the spot, make a circular motion toward the left shoulder, toward the outside, clockwise.

B. As your fingers are circling and pressing against the tender spot, make the following statement 3 times: "Even though,___[mis-belief statement]___, I totally and completely accept myself." An example would be: "Even though, I fear change, I totally and completely accept myself."

II. Tapping:

A. After the third time, tap the following 8 points repeating the [mis-belief statement] each time with each point. Tap each point 7 – 10 times:

1. The inner edge of the eyebrow just above the eye. [I fear change.]

2. Temple, just to the side of the eye. [I fear change.]

3. Just below the eye (on the cheekbone). [I fear change.]

4. Under the nose. [I fear change.]

5. Under the lips. [I fear change.]

6. Under the knob of the inside edge of the collar bone. [I fear change.]

7. 3" under the arm pit. [I fear change.]

8. Top back of the head. [I fear change.]

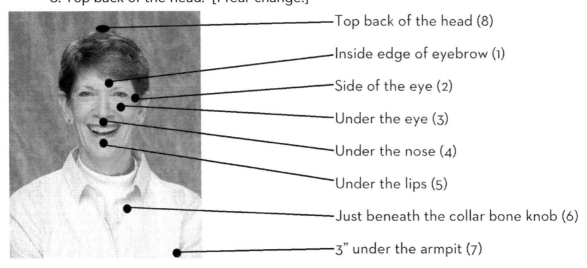

Top back of the head (8)

Inside edge of eyebrow (1)

Side of the eye (2)

Under the eye (3)

Under the nose (4)

Under the lips (5)

Just beneath the collar bone knob (6)

3" under the armpit (7)

B. After tapping, take a deep breath. If you are not able to take a deep, full, satisfying breath, do eye rolls.

III. Eye rolls

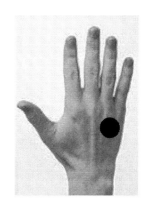

A. With one hand, tap continuously on the **back** of the other hand between the 4th and 5th fingers.
B. Head is held straight forward, eyes looking straight down.
C. For 6 seconds, roll your eyes from the floor straight up toward the ceiling while repeating the statement. Keep the head straight forward, only moving the eyes.

IV. Take another deep breath.

Karate Chop Point (KCP):

For the set up in EFT Tapping, use either the circling or the KCP. It is a matter of preference. One is not more effective than the other.

To tap the KCP, use the fingertips of the opposite hand or the KCP of both palms can be tapped together.

Tapping Points for the Short Form of EFT
Emotional Freedom Technique

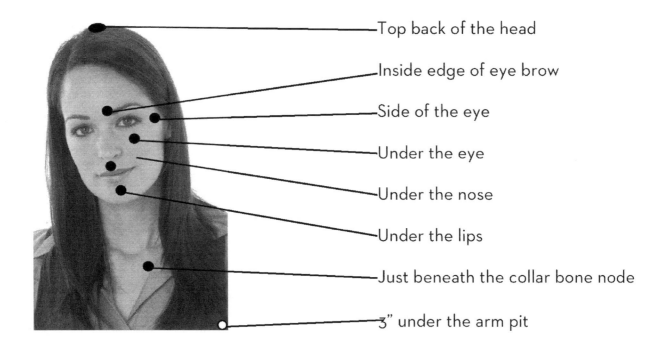

Top back of the head

Inside edge of eye brow

Side of the eye

Under the eye

Under the nose

Under the lips

Just beneath the collar bone node

3" under the arm pit

Yawning and Taking a Deep Breath

From Oriental medicine, we know that when Chi (energy) flows freely through the meridians, the body is healthy and balanced. Physical, mental, and/or emotional illness can result when the energy is blocked.

Dysfunctional beliefs and emotions produce blocks along the meridians, blocking energy from flowing freely in the body.

With EFT tapping, as we tap, we are releasing the blocks. As blocked energy is able to flow more freely, the body is now able to "breathe a sigh of relief." Yawning is that sigh of relief.

If, after tapping, we are able to take a complete, deep, full, and satisfying breath, we know that an EFT tapping statement has cleared. This yawn is an indication that an EFT tapping statement has cleared.

If the yawn or breath is not a full, deep breath then the statement didn't clear completely.

Integration...What Happens After Tapping

After tapping, our system needs some downtime for integration to take place. When the physical body and the mind are "idle," integration can then take place.

Sometimes, in the first 24 hours after tapping, we might find ourselves vegging more than normal, sleeping more than normal, or more tired than normal. This downtime is needed to integrate the new changes.

After installing a new program into our computer, sometimes we have to reboot the computer (shut down and restart) for the new program to be integrated into the system.

After tapping, our bodies need to reboot. We need some downtime. When we sleep, the new changes are integrated.

Healing begins naturally after the body has had a chance to integrate.

Sometimes after tapping, we forget the intensity of our pain and think that our feeling better had nothing to do with the tapping. Something so simple could not possibly create the improvement in our state of mind!

When we cut our finger, once it is healed, we don't even remember cutting our finger. As we move toward health, wealth, and well-being, sometimes we don't remember how unhappy, restless, or isolated we once felt.

How Does EFT Tapping Work?

1. Acceptance: The last part of the tapping statement we say, "I totally and completely accept myself." **Acceptance brings us into present time.** We can only heal if we are in present time. Laughter brings us into present time. "Laughter is the best medicine."

2. Addresses the current mis-belief on a subconscious level: In order to make changes in our lives, we have to change the dysfunctional beliefs, the mis-belief on a subconscious level. The middle part of the tapping statements are the "instructions" for the subconscious. **In order to make changes in our lives, we only care what the subconscious hears.**

3. Pattern interrupt: Dysfunctional memories and/or mis-beliefs disrupt or block the flow of energy from flowing freely along the meridians. Tapping is a pattern interrupt that disrupts the flow of energy to allow our **body's own Infinite Wisdom to come forth for healing.**

4. Mis-direct: One role of the physical body is to protect us. When our hand is too close to a flame, the body automatically pulls the hand back to safety. An EFT Tapping statement that agrees with the current belief is more effective. The physical body is less likely to "sabotage" the tapping if it agrees with the current belief.

An Example: The very first tapping statement we need to tap is: "It is not okay or safe for my life to change." Even though our lives are constantly changing does not mean we are comfortable or okay with change. When we are not comfortable with change, it creates stress for the body.

EFT Tapping Statement: "It is not okay or safe for my life to change."

* This statement appeases the physical body since it agrees with the current belief.
* The subconscious hears, "It is okay and safe for my life to change."
* The tapping disrupts the energy flow so our Truth can come forth.

The body will always gravitate to health, wealth, and well-being when the conditions allow it. EFT Tapping weeds the garden so that the blossoms can bloom more easily and effortlessly.

Science and EFT Tapping Research

EFT has been researched in more than 10 countries by more than 60 investigators whose results have been published in more than 20 different peer-reviewed journals. Two of the leading researchers are Dawson Church, Ph.D. and David Feinstein, Ph.D.

Dr. Dawson Church, a leading expert on energy psychology and an EFT master, has gathered all the research information and can be found on this website: www.EFTUniverse.com.

TWO RESEARCH STUDIES DISCUSSED BELOW

HARVARD MEDICAL SCHOOLS STUDIES AND THE BRAIN'S STRESS RESPONSE

Studies at the Harvard Medical School revealed that stimulating the body's meridian points significantly reduced activity in a part of the brain called the amygdala.

The amygdala can be thought of as the body's alarm system. When the body is experiencing trauma or fear, the amygdala is triggered and the body is flooded with cortisol also know as the "stress hormone." The stress response sets up an intricate chain reactions.

The studies showed that stimulating or tapping points along the meridians such as EFT tapping, drastically reduced and/or eliminated the stress response and the resulting chain reaction.

DR. DAWSON CHURCH AND CORTISOL REDUCTION

Another significant study was conducted by Dr. Dawson Church. He studied the impact an hour tapping session would have on the cortisol levels of 83 subjects. He also measured the cortisol levels of people who received traditional talk therapy and the cortisol levels of a third group who received no treatment at all.

On an average, for the 83 subjects that completed an hour tapping session, cortisol levels were reduced by 24% reduction. Some subjects experienced a 50% reduction in cortisol levels.

Subjects that completed an hour long traditional talk therapy and the subjects that had completed neither sessions did not experience any significant cortisol reduction.

Benefits of Using EFT Tapping

* The last part of the statement is "I totally and completely **accept** myself." **Acceptance** brings us into present time. Healing can only take place when we are in present time.

* By tapping, we are **calling forth our truths.** The key word here is **"our."** Not anyone else's. If my name is "Lucas," tapping the statement "Even though my name is Troy," my name will not be changed to Troy.

* Tapping **calls forth our own body's Infinite Wisdom.** When we cut our finger, our body knows how to heal the cut itself. Once the dysfunctional emotions, experiences, and beliefs have been "deleted," our body **automatically** gravitates to health, wealth, wisdom, peace, love, joy...

* By changing the mis-beliefs and dysfunctional emotions on a subconscious level, the changes we make with EFT are **permanent.**

* By tapping, we are **"neutralizing"** the stored memories that have been blocking energy from flowing freely along the meridians.

* Another benefit of tapping and EFT is desensitization. Let's say, we have a difficult person in our life that ignores us and/or criticizes us and we tap the statement: "This difficult person [or their name] ignores and criticizes me."

Tapping doesn't mean they will no longer ignore and/or criticize us.

It can, though, **desensitize us** so we no longer are affected by their behavior. Once we are desensitized, our perception and mental thinking improves. We are better able to make informed decisions. We don't take and make everything personally. Our health is not negatively impacted. Our heart doesn't beat 100 beats/minute. Smoke stops coming out of our ears. And our faces don't turn red with anger and frustration.

The Very First EFT Tapping Statement to Tap

The very first EFT tapping statement I have clients and students tap is "It is not okay or safe for my life to change." I have muscle tested this statement with more than a thousand people. Not one person tested strong that is was okay or safe for their life to change.

How effective can EFT or any therapy be if
it isn't okay or safe for our lives to change?

Since our lives are constantly changing, if it is not okay or safe for our lives to change, every time our lives change, it creates stress for the body. Stress creates another whole set of issues for ourselves, our lives, and our bodies.

IT'S NOT OKAY OR SAFE FOR MY LIFE TO CHANGE.

Intensity Level

One measure of knowing how much an "issue" has been "resolved" is to begin, before tapping, by giving the issue an intensity number between 1 – 10, with 10 being high.

For example, you want a romantic partnership yet, you haven't met "the one." Thinking about the likelihood of a romantic relationship happening for you, how likely, on a scale of 1 – 10, with 10 being very likely and 1, not likely at all, would a romantic relationship happen for you?

Okay. You gave yourself a 2. Now let's start tapping!

When asked what the "issues" might be, "Well," you say. "It doesn't seem as if the people I want, want me."

Great tapping statement. So, you tap out, "Even though, the people I want don't want me, I totally and completely accept myself." After tapping you check in with yourself, the Intensity Level (IL) has gone up to a 4, a little bit more likely.

What comes to mind now? You say, "No one will find me desirable." Great tapping statement. You tap out, "Even though, no one will find me desirable, I totally and completely accept myself." Check the IL. How likely? Now you are at a 5. Cool! Progress.

What comes to mind now? You say, "I'm not comfortable being vulnerable in romantic relationships." Great tapping statement. You tap out, "Even though, I'm not comfortable being vulnerable in a romantic relationship, I totally and completely accept myself." Check the IL. Now it is a 6. Still progress.

What comes to mind now? "Well, it feels like if I am in a relationship, I will lose a lot of my freedom." Make this into a tapping statements. "Even though, I will lose my freedom when I am in a relationship, I totally and completely accept myself." The IL has gone up to a 7.

What comes to mind now? "Oh, if I was in a relationship, I would have to be accountable to someone!" Make this into a tapping statement: "Even though, I would have to be accountable to someone if I was in a relationship, I totally and completely accept myself." Wow...the IL is 9, very likely!

GIVING AN ISSUE AN INTENSITY LEVEL GIVES US AN INDICATION OF THE PROGRESS WE ARE MAKING WITH RESOLVING AND/OR HEALING THAT ISSUE IN OUR LIVES.

Using a Negative EFT Tapping Statement

Our beliefs **precede** all of our thoughts, feelings, decisions, choices, actions, reactions, and experiences...

If we want to make changes in our lives, we have to change the mis-beliefs, the dysfunctional beliefs. Our beliefs are stored in the subconscious.

To change our lives, to change a belief, we only care what the subconscious hears when we tap. The subconscious does not hear the word "no." When we say, "I am not going to eat that piece of cake," the subconscious hears, "Yummm, cake!"

Example, if we don't believe we had what it takes to be successful and we tap the statement, "I have what it takes to be successful," the body could sabotage the tapping. We could tap and it won't clear.

If instead the statement we make is "I don't have what it takes to be successful," the **"not"** appeases the physical body and the subconscious hears, "I have what it takes to be successful!"

A statement with the word "no" or "not," although may seem to be contradictory, works best!

Finishing Touches (Optional)

If we tap a statement that the body knows not to be true, the tapping statement may not clear. As discussed with the Affirmation section on page 27, first we need to tap the affirmation with the "no" inserted in the tapping statement.

Part 1 of Finishing Touches - Read the statements on the following page. If one or more of the statements doesn't feel true yet, then you might want to do one round of the statements by inserting a "no" into the statement.

Part 2 - Some like to finish their tapping with statements that are centering and calming. If this is you, then you might want to try the 16 statements below and/or make up those that you like. The statements below can be said in any order that works for you.

Tapping Location	Statement
Eyebrow	All is well in my life.
Temple	Every day in every way I am getting better and better.
Under the Eye	I am fulfilled in every way, every day.
Under the Nose	My blessings appears in rich appropriate form with divine timing.
Under the Lips	I am an excellent steward of wealth and am blessed with great abundance.
Under the Collarbone Knob	I take complete responsibility for everything in my life.
Under the Arm	I have all the tools, skills, and abilities to excel in my life.
Top back part of the Head	I know I will be able to handle anything that arises in my life.
Eyebrow	All my dreams, hopes, wishes, and goals are being fulfilled each and every day.
Temple	Divine love expressing through me, now draws to me new ideas.
Under the Eye	I am comfortable with my life changing.
Under the Nose	I am able to create all that I desire.
Under the Lips	I know what needs to be done and follow through to completion.
Under the Collarbone Knob	My health is perfect in every way, physically, mentally, emotionally, and spiritually.
Under the Arm	I invite into my subconscious Archangel Raphael to heal all that needs to be forgiven, released, and redeemed. Cleanse me and free me from it now.
Top back part of the Head	The light of God surrounds me. The love of God enfolds me. The power of God protects me. The presence of God watches over and flows through me.

How to Use This Book

1. The statements are divided into sections. Read through the statements in one section. As you read a statement, notice if you have any reaction to the statement or feel the statement might be true for you. If so, note the number for that statement.

2. Once you have completed reading all the statements in one section, go back and reread the statements you noted and rate them on a scale of 1 – 10, with 10 being a biggie."

3. List the top statements.

4. From this list, select one and describe how it plays out in your life. It is important to recognize and identify the pattern. What are the consequences of having this mis-belief? Is there a trigger? How does it begin? How does it benefit you? How has it harmed you? There will be a different example listed in each section.

5. Tap out the statements. Statements can be combined for scripts...a different statement on each of the different tapping points in one round of tapping.

6. Describe any flashbacks or memories that you might have had as you were tapping out the statements. Describe any ah-has, insights, and/or thoughts you might have had as a result of tapping the statements.

7. After tapping all the statements, review them to determine if you still have a reaction to any of the statements. If you do, you have several options. One, put a "Why" before the statement. Tap out the answer. Secondly, note that this statement may not have cleared and continue on to the next section. Most likely, after additional statements are tapped, statements that may not have cleared, will clear without having to tap the statement again.

8. Allow some downtime for integration and for the body to heal.

9. The number of sections you do at a time will be up to you. Initially, you might want to do one section to determine if you get tired and need to have some downtime after tapping.

10. The day after tapping, again review the statements you tapped to determine if you still have a reaction. If you do, follow the instructions in #7.

1 – 20 EFT Tapping Statements

Money is a thought form. It is a symbol of energy and as such it has no real, intrinsic value. It is neither good nor bad, positive nor evil. It is impartial.

Stuart Wilde

1. I spend everything I earn.

2. I cannot excel financially.

3. I will never be prosperous.

4. I am angry that I have debt.

5. I spend money I don't have.

6. I resent people that are rich.

7. I live paycheck to paycheck.

8. Money is scarce and limited.

9. I use money to please others.

10. There is never enough money.

11. I cannot live within my means.

12. I must work hard my entire life.

13. I lack the wisdom to be wealthy.

14. I am unconscious of my spending.

15. It is greedy to ask for what I want.

16. I have to work hard for my money.

17. I don't have the courage to be rich.

18. I am not willing to invest in myself.

19. My financial life will never be easy.

20. My efforts will never *create* wealth.

Journaling Pages for Statements 1 – 20

Money doesn't change men. It merely unmasks them. If a man is naturally selfish or arrogant or greedy, the money brings that out.

Henry Ford

1. From the tapping statements between 1 – 20, list the top seven statements that you thought or felt applied to you:

1.

2.

3.

4.

5.

6.

7.

2. From this list of seven statements, select one and describe how it plays out in your life. Give an example or two. It is important to recognize and identify the pattern. Is there a trigger? How does it begin? How has it benefited you? How has it harmed you? For instance, do you have the courage to be rich? 75% of people that become instant millionaires file for bankruptcy within 5 years of their windfall. It takes courage to manage wealth. Would you end up giving all your wealthy away because you don't have the courage to be wealthy?

3. Tap out the top 7 statements.

4. As you were tapping out the statements, did you have any flashback or memories of the past, any additional insights, and/or ah-ha thoughts? If so, write them down. Make note of them.

21 – 40 EFT Tapping Statements

For a man to achieve all that is demanded of him,
he must regard himself as greater than he is.

Unknown

21. I have to work for everything in life.

22. Wealth is synonymous with struggle.

23. My efforts will never *produce* wealth.

24. I don't handle money like a grown-up.

25. I must work really hard for my money.

26. Having money solves all my problems.

27. I don't know where I spend my money.

28. It is not okay/safe for me to be wealthy.

29. Prosperity is a block to spiritual growth.

30. I am envious of other's financial wealth.

31. Spirituality is synonymous with poverty.

32. I will never be given any financial breaks.

33. I will always be broke no matter what I do.

34. Money runs through my fingers like water.

35. It is hopeless that I will ever be prosperous.

36. I will never be rich enough to get out of debt.

37. I will never be successful in regard to money.

38. It is not okay for me to have more than I need.

39. My self-image is one of poverty not prosperity.

40. Debt is a condition of life that seldom changes.

Journaling Pages for Statements 21 – 40

If you are going through hell, keep going.

Rob Estes

1. From the tapping statements between 1 – 20, list the top seven statements that you thought or felt applied to you:

1.

2.

3.

4.

5.

6.

7.

2. From this list of seven statements, select one and describe how it plays out in your life. Give an example or two. It is important to recognize and identify the pattern. Is there a trigger? How does it begin? How has it benefited you? How has it harmed you? For instance, do you handle money like a grown-up? Being a grown-up means responsible for all your decisions and choices, including your financial choices. Do you know where your money goes? Do you know how much it cost to support yourself? Or is it easier to charge, amass debit then file for bankruptcy?

3. Tap out the top 7 statements.

4. As you were tapping out the statements, did you have any flashback or memories of the past, any additional insights, and/or ah-ha thoughts? If so, write them down. Make note of them.

41 – 60 EFT Tapping Statements

The trouble with life is, we are half way through it before we realize it's a "do it yourself" thing.

Annie Zadra

41. I am inferior to others.

42. Survival is my only identity.

43. I will never be good enough.

44. I often feel inferior to others.

45. My self-worth is non-existent.

46. I have to do, do, do to survive.

47. I have no inner sense of worth.

48. I have to work hard to survive.

49. Life is full of traps and threats.

50. I worry about financial matters.

51. I live in a constant state of fear.

52. I am defective, damaged goods.

53. I am drowning in my depression.

54. I am overly sensitive to criticism.

55. "Just do it," doesn't work for me.

56. Life is one problem after another.

57. Life is frightening and intimidating.

58. Nothing ever turns out right for me.

59. It is not okay/safe to put myself first.

60. I am full of self-doubt and insecurity.

Journaling Pages for Statements 41 – 60

The truth is that our finest moments are most likely to occur when we are feeling deeply uncomfortable, unhappy, or unfulfilled. For it is only in such moments, propelled by our discomfort, that we are likely to step out of our ruts and start searching for different ways or truer answers.

M. Scott Peck

1. From the tapping statements between 1 – 20, list the top seven statements that you thought or felt applied to you:

1.

2.

3.

4.

5.

6.

7.

2. From this list of seven statements, select one and describe how it plays out in your life. Give an example or two. It is important to recognize and identify the pattern. Is there a trigger? How does it begin? How has it benefited you? How has it harmed you? For instance, do you turn small personal flaws into major catastrophes? Why might that be? To feel sorry for yourself? To discourage yourself from learning any new tools and skills to be successful? To prove you are a failure? To avoid something you don't want to do? Fear?

3. Tap out the top 7 statements.

4. As you were tapping out the statements, did you have any flashback or memories of the past, any additional insights, and/or ah-ha thoughts? If so, write them down. Make note of them.

61 – 80 EFT Tapping Statements

Man cannot discover new oceans unless he has courage to lose sight of the shore.

Andre Gide

61. I second-guess every decision I make.

62. I'm not able to move beyond survival.

63. I don't know how to handle my anger.

64. No matter what I do I can't get ahead.

65. I must rescue those that need my help.

66. I am sinking in the quicksand of despair.

67. I say "yes" when I would rather say "no."

68. It's not safe to reveal the real me to others.

69. I don't know who I am outside of survival.

70. I'm disappointed the way my life unfolded.

71. I'm paralyzed and unable to move forward.

72. I am constantly comparing myself to others.

73. My life didn't turn out as I thought it would.

74. I am overwhelmed with the task of surviving.

75. It's not okay for me to have more than others.

76. It is not okay/safe to move forward in my life.

77. I feel overwhelmed, defeated, and victimized.

78. I focus on the negative instead of the positive.

79. My life lacks meaning, purpose, and direction.

80. I am super-sensitive to criticism and rejection.

Journaling Pages for Statements 61 – 80

The greatest achievement was at first and for a time a dream.
The oak sleeps in the acorn, the bird waits in the egg, and in the highest vision
of the soul a waking angel stirs. Dreams are the seedlings of realities.

James Allen

1. From the tapping statements between 1 – 20, list the top seven statements that you thought or felt applied to you:

1.

2.

3.

4.

5.

6.

7.

2. From this list of seven statements, select one and describe how it plays out in your life. Give an example or two. It is important to recognize and identify the pattern. Is there a trigger? How does it begin? How has it benefited you? How has it harmed you? For instance, do you feel your future is hopeless? Is it easier to feel hopeless than to do the work necessary to make your life a masterpiece?

3. Tap out the top 7 statements.

4. As you were tapping out the statements, did you have any flashback or memories of the past, any additional insights, and/or ah-ha thoughts? If so, write them down. Make note of them.

EFT Tapping Statements 81 – 100

The ultimate measure of a man is not where he stands in moments of comfort and convenience, but where he stands in times of challenge and controversy.

Dr. Martin Luther King, Jr.

81. I don't believe in myself.

82. I am afraid of the unknown.

83. I lack the courage to act now.

84. I hide my fears from everyone.

85. I cannot accept myself as I am.

86. I avoid confrontation at all cost.

87. I lack the courage to take action.

88. I have difficulty making decisions.

89. I find it difficult to give up control.

90. I lack the courage to be prosperous.

91. I engage in self-defeating behaviors.

92. I am defeated by the obstacles of life.

93. I feel defeated, hopeless, and trapped.

94. I agonized over every decision I make.

95. I lack goals and a direction for my life.

96. My self-talk is judgmental and critical.

97. I lack the confidence to be courageous.

98. I don't have the courage to live my life.

99. I am paralyzed by the challenges of life.

100. I cannot cope with the challenges of life.

Journaling Page for Statements 81 – 100

A kite flies best when the wind blows in one direction and the string pulls from another.

Henry Ford

1. From the tapping statements between 1 – 20, list the top seven statements that you thought or felt applied to you:

1.

2.

3.

4.

5.

6.

7.

2. From this list of seven statements, select one and describe how it plays out in your life. Give an example or two. It is important to recognize and identify the pattern. Is there a trigger? How does it begin? How has it benefited you? How has it harmed you? For instance, do you have difficulties facing your fears? Do you use fear as the excuse not to grow, not to live your life, to hide, and/or to be lazy?

3. Tap out the top 7 statements.

4. As you were tapping out the statements, did you have any flashback or memories of the past, any additional insights, and/or ah-ha thoughts? If so, write them down. Make note of them.

EFT Tapping Statements 101 – 120

Courage is doing what you're afraid to do. There can be no courage unless you're scared.
Eddie Rickenbacker

101. My courage has been tested and I failed.

102. I lack the determination to be courageous.

103. My life lacks joy, laughter, and happiness.

104. I am plagued with "should" and "have to."

105. I don't have the wisdom to be courageous.

106. My fears are stronger than my convictions.

107. The word courage is not in my vocabulary.

108. My life lacks wonder, enthusiasm, and joy.

109. My courage has atrophied from lack of use.

110. Being courageous is not a way of life for me.

111. My superwoman/superman cape is worn out.

112. No matter how much I do, it is never enough.

113. I don't know how to use fear to my advantage.

114. It takes more courage to be wealthy than I have.

115. I don't have the courage to live a congruent life.

116. I don't face conflicts with grace and confidence.

117. I am not committed to myself, my growth, to me.

118. I don't have the courage to give up my addiction.

119. I allow others to violate my limits and boundaries.

120. Others think I am selfish for putting my needs first.

Journaling Page for Statements 101 – 120

Hiding in my room, safe within my womb, I touch no one and no one touches me.
I am a rock, I am an island. And a rock feels no pain; And an island never cries.

Paul Simon
I Am a Rock (song)

1. From the tapping statements between 1 – 20, list the top seven statements that you thought or felt applied to you:

1.

2.

3.

4.

5.

6.

7.

2. From this list of seven statements, select one and describe how it plays out in your life. Give an example or two. It is important to recognize and identify the pattern. Is there a trigger? How does it begin? How has it benefited you? How has it harmed you? For instance, it takes courage to be committed to yourself and your growth. Do you fully live your life or are you afraid of making mistakes? Can you learn from your mistakes? Can you find the silver lining around challenges?

3. Tap out the top 7 statements.

4. As you were tapping out the statements, did you have any flashback or memories of the past, any additional insights, and/or ah-ha thoughts? If so, write them down. Make note of them.

EFT Tapping Statements 121 - 140

Trust, integrity, and gratitude, these are the foundation upon which we should build our lives.
We do not need anyone else for any of these. If we learn to trust ourselves,
we will know truth. If we are honest with ourselves, we will know integrity.
If we are thankful for all that is, we will know love.

Tessa Cason

121. Poor people are powerless.

122. I quit before the extra mile.

123. I give in to what others want.

124. I'm powerless and defenseless.

125. Being powerful is too stressful.

126. I'm too insecure to be powerful.

127. I take and make things personal.

128. I don't know how to be powerful.

129. Only rich people can be powerful.

130. Being powerful makes me a target.

131. I am too judgmental to be powerful.

132. I produce excuses rather than results.

133. I lack the self-esteem to be powerful.

134. I quit if I don't succeed the first time.

135. I'm not smart enough to be powerful.

136. I'm too much of a critic to be powerful.

137. I'm not talented enough to be powerful.

138. Powerful people are ruthless and driven.

139. I allow myself to be controlled by others.

140. I don't know how to set or achieve goals.

Journaling Page for Statements 121 – 140

Most of our limitations are self-imposed. Roger Bannister was the first human to run a sub-four-minute mile, a barrier that was previously deemed insurmountable. Immediately after Bannister proved it was "possible," runners all over the world repeated his feat.

Bob Moward

1. From the tapping statements between 1 – 20, list the top seven statements that you thought or felt applied to you:

1.

2.

3.

4.

5.

6.

7.

2. From this list of seven statements, select one and describe how it plays out in your life. Give an example or two. It is important to recognize and identify the pattern. Is there a trigger? How does it begin? How has it benefited you? How has it harmed you? For instance, do you focus more on your weaknesses than your strengths? Would it appear bragging and arrogant if you focused on your strengths? Or do you truly believe you have no strengths, that you are totally and completely flawed and damaged goods? Do you focus on what you don't have or what you do have?

3. Tap out the top 7 statements.

4. As you were tapping out the statements, did you have any flashback or memories of the past, any additional insights, and/or ah-ha thoughts? If so, write them down. Make note of them.

EFT Tapping Statements 141 –160

No one can defeat us unless we first defeat ourselves.

Dwight D. Eisenhower

141. I lack the financial wealth to be powerful.

142. I am too critical of myself to be powerful.

143. I make too many mistakes to be powerful.

144. My life is too busy, scattered, and chaotic.

145. I don't believe that I can ever be powerful.

146. I don't know how to release my negativity.

147. I would rather stay naïve than be powerful.

148. I lack strategic, verbal, and language skills.

149. It is beyond my capabilities to be powerful.

150. Powerful people are overbearing and cruel.

151. Powerful people are unloving and uncaring.

152. Power is synonymous with battle and attack.

153. Others will not love me when I am powerful.

154. I would be laughed at if I tried to be powerful.

155. I allow others to rob me of my energy and time.

156. No one would ever believe that I was powerful.

157. The whole of me is scattered into bits of pieces.

158. Only power-hungry people want to be powerful.

159. Other people will challenge me if I am powerful.

160. I don't know how to turn my dreams into reality.

Journaling Page for Statements 141 – 160

People are like guided missiles. Without a target, they wander aimlessly across the horizons and eventually self-destruct.

Edge Keynote

1. From the tapping statements between 1 – 20, list the top seven statements that you thought or felt applied to you:

1.

2.

3.

4.

5.

6.

7.

2. From this list of seven statements, select one and describe how it plays out in your life. Give an example or two. It is important to recognize and identify the pattern. Is there a trigger? How does it begin? How has it benefited you? How has it harmed you? For instance, do you believe you will never have the things you want? Is this because you don't work toward their achievement, you are undeserving, and/or they are unrealistic?

3. Tap out the top 7 statements.

4. As you were tapping out the statements, did you have any flashback or memories of the past, any additional insights, and/or ah-ha thoughts? If so, write them down. Make note of them.

EFT Tapping Statements 161 – 180

*Always bear in mind that your own resolution to succeed
is more important than any other one thing.*

Abraham Lincoln

161. I don't expect to succeed.

162. I don't have faith in my ideas.

163. I'm stuck in analysis paralysis.

164. My identity is that of a failure.

165. I don't recover from my setbacks.

166. Only rich people can be successful.

167. I lack the confidence to be successful.

168. I lack the persistence to be successful.

169. I lack the self-esteem to be successful.

170. I'm not smart enough to be successful.

171. I lack the commitment to be successful.

172. I give up when obstacles block my way.

173. I've given up on my dreams and myself.

174. I can't figure out what I am doing wrong.

175. Money changes everything and everyone.

176. Success is the answer to all my problems.

177. I am not deserving and worthy of success.

178. Being successful would make me a target.

179. It is not okay/safe for me to be successful.

180. I don't have what it takes to be successful.

Journaling Page for Statements 161 - 180

*You cannot make footprints in the sands of time if you are sitting on your butt
and who wants to make butt prints in the sand of time?*

Bob Moawad

1. From the tapping statements between 1 – 20, list the top seven statements that you thought or felt applied to you:

1.

2.

3.

4.

5.

6.

7.

2. From this list of seven statements, select one and describe how it plays out in your life. Give an example or two. It is important to recognize and identify the pattern. Is there a trigger? How does it begin? How has it benefited you? How has it harmed you? For instance, do you really not have the energy to change your life or do you not have a compelling future to move toward? Do you not have the energy to fulfill your goals or do you not have any goals? Do you not have the energy to succeed or is it safer to fail?

3. Tap out the top 7 statements.

4. As you were tapping out the statements, did you have any flashback or memories of the past, any additional insights, and/or ah-ha thoughts? If so, write them down. Make note of them.

EFT Tapping Statements 181 – 200

There are no secrets to success.
It is the result of preparation, hard work, and learning from failure.

Colin Powell

181. I don't acknowledge my accomplishments.

182. I don't know how to strategize for success.

183. Only the strong and powerful can succeed.

184. I don't know how to get to there from here.

185. It is gloating to acknowledge my successes.

186. I don't believe that I can ever be successful.

187. Being successful is stressful and exhausting.

188. Successful people are overbearing and cruel.

189. I don't know how to deal with loss or defeat.

190. People will dislike me when I am successful.

191. I don't know how to overcome loss or defeat.

192. I lack the determination to keep on keeping on.

193. My goals are not within my realm of capability.

194. I cannot overcome my defects and deficiencies.

195. Success is synonymous with happily-ever-after.

196. Successful people are mean, rude, and uncaring.

197. I don't have the tools and skills to be successful.

198. I am not committed to making my goals a reality.

199. My identity is that of "struggle" and not of success.

200. I am not willing to stretch beyond my comfort zone.

Journaling Page for Statements 181 – 200

The road to success has many tempting parking places.

Steve Potter

1. From the tapping statements between 1 – 20, list the top seven statements that you thought or felt applied to you:

1.

2.

3.

4.

5.

6.

7.

2. From this list of seven statements, select one and describe how it plays out in your life. Give an example or two. It is important to recognize and identify the pattern. Is there a trigger? How does it begin? How has it benefited you? How has it harmed you? For instance, by believing you are defective, you really don't have to identify your goals, work toward their fulfillment, handle failure, learn new skills, or deal with adversity. What would happen if you thought of yourself as AWESOME!

3. Tap out the top 7 statements.

4. As you were tapping out the statements, did you have any flashback or memories of the past, any additional insights, and/or ah-ha thoughts? If so, write them down. Make note of them.

Loser vs Winners

Losers always have an excuse.
Winners always have an idea.

Losers fix the blame.
Winners fix the situation.

Losers make promises.
Winners keep commitments.

Losers let it happen.
Winners make it happen.

Losers identify with problems.
Winners identify with solutions.

Losers say "It isn't my fault."
Winners say "Let me help you."

Losers see a problem for every answer.
Winners see an answer for every problem.

Losers are down on life and high on drugs.
Winners are high on life and down on drugs.

Losers see the thunderstorms and icy streets.
Winners see rainbows and ice skates.

Losers are failure conscious.
Winners are success conscious.

Losers say "It might be possible but it's too difficult."
Winners say "It might be difficult, but it's possible."

Losers step on flowers in search of weeds.
Winners pull up weeds while enjoying the fragrance of the flowers.

Losers say, "Why don't they do something?"
Winners say, "Here's something I can do."

Dennis Waitley

About the Creator of the Program
Author – Tessa Cason, MA

I have been fortunate to have had a number of successful professional lives. In each of these endeavors, it provided the opportunity to observe someone's behavior, actions, reactions, habits, thoughts, feelings, choices, and decisions. Understanding who we are, how we became who we are, and how to change into who we want to become has been a fascinating area of study and research for me for 50 years.

As a swim coach and instructor of 10 and under kids, I had the opportunity to teach and train small children. As an instructor of PE at San Diego State University and Grossmont College, I had the opportunity to interact with and teach college-age individuals. As an owner of a gift company, I had the opportunity to work with business professionals. Belonging to a breakfast group called The Inside Edge and staffing events for The Learning Annex, I was able to interact with and observe the elite authors, speakers, and politicians. Managing a medical clinic provided the opportunity to interact with and observe the seriously ill, some terminal.

In 1977, as a hobby, I started a company that manufactured greeting cards and stationery. Eight years later, my company was grossing a million dollars in sale/year on 50 cent greeting cards.

When my business was grossing a million dollars in sale, I purchased a newly constructed townhouse in La Jolla. Unbeknownst to me, a natural gas pipe was severed during construction and not properly repaired. The gas leak went undetected for 2 1/2 years, 850 days. By then, my health was permanently damaged.

After the gas leak was discovered, all the doctors told me I would be environmentally ill for the rest of my life and would never be able to participate or function in the real world. Not believing the doctors, I set upon a course to discover alternative health treatments. Several years later, while still working on my health, I was managing an alternative health clinic. While working at the clinic, I was able to make the correlation between a patient's emotions and beliefs with their physical illnesses.

In 1996, after thirty years of book reading, psychology classes, metaphysical classes, lectures, and observation, I applied my knowledge and skills into a life coaching practice. I thoroughly enjoyed being a Transformational Life Coach, helping others find clarity in their lives.

Only one problem. It was this: The clients were not completing their assigned tasks that together we had decided they would do as their homework. Even though the clients knew what to do and wanted to do the tasks, somehow the tasks were not getting completed.

Knowing that all of our actions and reactions, thoughts and feelings, choices and decisions are based on our beliefs, I went searching for a tool that would change dysfunctional beliefs. I visited a friend that managed a bookstore and told her my dilemma and that I was in need of a tool, process, or technique that would change dysfunctional beliefs. She reached for a book that was on the counter, informing me that this new addition for them was flying off the shelves and their customers were raving about. It was a book on EFT (Emotional Freedom Technique) Tapping.

I read the book and ordered the videos. Even though I was intrigued, I had no clue how tapping my head could change dysfunctional beliefs or our lives. I had some adventuresome clients (and forgiving if need be) that I taught how to tap.

When every single client returned for their next appointment and shared how different their lives had been that week because of tapping, I took notice! My curiosity was peaked. I then put a lot of time and energy into figuring out how this powerful transformational tool, EFT Tapping, worked and how to best utilize EFT Tapping.

I soon realized working with my clients that the most important aspect of EFT Tapping was the statement that is said as we tap. I also realized that some of the statements I wrote up for one client could be used for another. My clients wanted homework, wanted tapping statements to do on their own. I started a library of EFT Tapping statements that I wrote out for my client as their homework.

In 2005 I was diagnosed with thyroid cancer. While researching thyroid cancer, I discovered that 20 years after exposure to natural gas, thyroid issues would result. It was 20 years nearly to the month that I started having thyroid issues.

From the time I was diagnosed and had surgery, those 6 weeks I only focused on the emotional issues associated with the thyroid and tapped. I did not pursue any other treatments, supplements, or therapies in the 6 weeks leading up to the surgery other than EFT Tapping.

In the recovery room after surgery, the surprised doctor told me that even though two different labs came back with the diagnoses of cancer, it was not cancer. I knew the tapping had changed the energy of the cancer and it no longer was cancer.

Our lives don't change until we change our programming...the beliefs on a subconscious level. EFT Tapping is one of the most powerful techniques I found that could do just that: change our beliefs on a subconscious level.

After surgery, knowing the power of EFT Tapping, knowing the significance of the tapping statement, and knowing that beliefs precede all of our thoughts and feelings, choices and decisions, actions, reactions, and experiences, I created 43 Books for Practitioners and 43 Workbooks for Everyone that were filled with mis-belief, dysfunctional EFT tapping statements.

I am revamping the Workbooks. In the revamped Workbooks, I am combining tapping statements for 5 different topics in each theme-book to heal the issue as completely as possible.

I also have a series of "EFT Tapping Statement" Kindle eBooks on Amazon.

My two greatest joys are helping those that want to grow, evolve, and transform their lives and train others to be transformational coaches!

Books and Kindles eBooks by Tessa Cason

80 EFT TAPPING STATEMENTS FOR:
Abandonment
Abundance, Wealth, Money
Addictions
Adult Children of Alcoholics
Anger and Frustration
Anxiety and Worry
Change
"Less Than" and Anxiety
Manifesting a Romantic Relationship
Relationship with Self
Self Esteem
Social Anxiety
Weight and Emotional Eating

100 EFT Tapping Statements for Accepting Our Uniqueness and Being Different
100 EFT Tapping Statements for Fear of Computers
100 EFT Tapping Statements for I'm Not Extraordinary!
200 EFT Tapping Statements for Healing a Broken Heart
200 EFT Tapping Statements for Knowing God
200 EFT Tapping Statements for Procrastination
200 EFT Tapping Statements for PTSD
200 EFT Tapping Statements for Wealth
240 EFT Tapping Statements for Fear
300 EFT Tapping Statements for Healing the Self
300 EFT Tapping Statements for Dealing with Obnoxious People
340 EFT Tapping Statements for Healing From the Loss of a Loved One
400 EFT Tapping Statements for Being a Champion
400 EFT Tapping Statements for Dreams to Reality
400 EFT Tapping Statements for My Thyroid Story
500 EFT Tapping Statements for Moving Out of Survival
700 EFT Tapping Statements for Weight, Emotional Eating, and Food Cravings
All Things EFT Tapping Manual
Emotional Significance of Human Body Parts

Muscle Testing - Obstacles and Helpful Hints
EFT TAPPING STATEMENTS FOR:
A Broken Heart, Abandonment, Anger, Depression, Grief, Emotional Healing
Anxiety, Fear, Anger, Self Pity, Change
Champion, Success, Personal Power, Self Confidence, Leader/Role Model
PTSD, Disempowered, Survival, Fear, Anger
Weight & Food Cravings, Anger, Grief, Not Good Enough, Failure

OTHER BOOKS
Why we Crave What We Crave: The Archetypes of Food Cravings
How to Heal Our Food Cravings

EFT WORKBOOK AND JOURNAL FOR EVERYONE:
Abandonment
Abundance, Money, Prosperity
Addictions
Adult Children of Alcoholics
Anger, Apathy, Guilt
Anxiety/Worry
Being A Man
Being, Doing, Belonging
Champion
Change
Conflict
Courage
Dark Forces
Decision Making
Depression
Difficult/Toxic Parents
Difficult/Toxic People
Emotional Healing
Fear
Forgiveness
God
Grief
Happiness/Joy
Intuition
Leadership
Live Your Dreams

Life Purpose/Mission
People Pleaser
Perfectionism
Personal Power
Relationship w/Others
Relationship w/Self & Commitment to Self
Self Confidence
Self Worth/Esteem
Sex
Shame
Stress
Success
Survival
Transitions
Trust/Discernment
Victim, Self-pity, Self-Defeating Behavior, Shadow Self
Weight and Emotional Eating

MIS-BELIEF EFT STATEMENTS FOR PRACTITIONERS:

Abandonment
Abundance, Money, Prosperity
Addictions
Adult Children of Alcoholics
Anger, Apathy, Guilt
Anxiety/Worry
Being A Man
Being, Doing, Belonging
Champion
Change
Conflict
Courage
Dark Forces
Decision Making
Depression
Difficult/Toxic Parents
Difficult/Toxic People
Emotional Healing
Fear
Forgiveness
God
Grief

Happiness/Joy
Intuition
Leadership
Live Your Dreams
Life Purpose/Mission
People Pleaser
Perfectionism
Personal Power
Relationship w/Others
Relationship w/Self & Commitment w/Self
Self Confidence
Self Worth/Esteem
Sex
Shame
Stress
Success
Survival
Transitions
Trust/Discernment
Victim, Self-pity, Self-Defeating Behavior, Shadow Self
Weight and Emotional Eating

With Gratitude and Appreciation

There are several people I would like to thank:

* I am thankful for Roger Callahan's, Gary Craig's, and Pat Carrington's work developing TFT and EFT. Without their willingness to break the mold, we might still be lying on the couch telling our stories rather than healing our hearts and mis-beliefs.

* I am very thankful for my clients in 2000 that were willing to try something new, something untested, something that was outside the norm. I learned so much watching their growth and evolution.

* I am thankful for Nick Ortner and The Tapping Solution. Nick is willing to defend EFT Tapping and brave the way for the rest of us.

* I am thankful for the research that Dawson Church has put into legitimizing EFT Tapping.

* I am thankful for all the practitioners and people that believe and continue to tap even though it is not quite widely accepted yet.

The End

Printed in Great Britain
by Amazon